I DIDN'T SIGN UP FOR ALL THIS!

I DIDN'T SIGN UP FOR ALL THIS!

KEM & DARA GASKIN

CONFESSIONS
PUBLISHING

I Didn't Sign Up for All This!

Copyright © 2019 by Kem & Dara Gaskin

ISBN: 978-1-7334723-3-3

Printed and bound in the United States of America.

Editor: Maria Stokes

Confessions Publishing is a subsidiary of Roszien Kay LLC, Lancaster, CA 93536. For information regarding discounts on bulk purchase and all other inquiries, please contact the author directly at authorsgaskin@gmail.com

We want to thank our Heavenly Father, our Lord Jesus Christ, and the Precious Holy Spirit for so graciously helping us through so many battles and many situations in our life.

Without you our God, we would not be who we are today! "If it had not been the Lord on our side we would have perished" (Psalm 124)

With great Honor we dedicate this book to You, our Merciful, Loving, Faithful and Gracious God! Father be glorified and use this book to strengthen, encourage, and bless every reader! In Jesus' Name!!!

CONTENTS

PREFACE

Lord I know you've called me, but I didn't sign up for all this!

If you've ever said anything like this before, then you're not alone. We've been there multiple times and many others have also!

There are times when you're just loving God, minding your own business, doing the will of God, then all of a sudden something unexpected happens. You have faith, you have vision, you're doing your best to obey the call of God, then suddenly "betrayal, hurt, disappointments, money problems, family problems, church or business problems."

It might even seem like multiple warheads were shot at you all at one time.

Sometimes things will arise within us that we didn't even know were there, like roots of fear, insecurities, or weaknesses that God says now it's time to burn those things out of you so you can experience more freedom. God will use the fire also to prepare us more for His calling! Wait Lord I said yes to walking with you, being a friend of God & winning millions of souls around the world. But all this other stuff "Lord I didn't sign up for all this."

If that's you then you're in good company. Abraham, Isaac, Jacob, Joseph, Esther, Daniel, Our King Jesus, Peter, Paul & more said "Yes" to the call of God, but after they said "Yes" they went through many adversities. The bible is clear ". . . In the world you will have tribulation" (John 16:33). But Jesus said "be of good cheer, I have overcome the world" (*id*).

You're a spiritual warrior, not a wimp. You're more than a conqueror in Christ Jesus (Romans 8:37). Greater is He that lives in you, than he that is in the world (1 John 4:4). The hurts, betrayals, and trials you're going through will all pass away, but if you keep your heart pure before God, you'll be like Joseph that although he went through much hardship, there came a time that God's word came to pass (Psalm 105:19).

We declare that you will experience God's Word come to pass in your life. By God's grace you won't quit but you will be strong, trust God, keep your heart pure and experience God's supernatural grace to empower you to stay the course and finish your race!!! Love never fails and oh how your Heavenly Father loves you!

Through our many trials, hurts, betrayals, disappointments and more our Father in Heaven has never failed us. We wrote this book to encourage you that you're not alone. Great things are ahead of you, be strong, don't quit, keep moving and never compromise.

In the following pages we pray you will find strength, encouragement, wisdom, comfort and vision to fulfill your destiny!

CHAPTER I
THE CALL/ YOUR DESTINY

◆

Just because you've gone through one test to another, one battle to another, or one hurt to another, doesn't mean something is wrong with you. Matter of fact I sense the need to declare over you "There's nothing wrong with you, but rather, you're called!"

You're called by God! God the Father put you on this planet with "powerful gifts, talents and abilities" and He predestined you to a specific assignment! You're not just roaming through life. The Father God has marked you, called you and ordained you before you were born "for such a time as this."

Your generation is waiting for you to show up and display the greatness of God! Now is the time. God has shifted the earth and there is a new breed of sons and daughters arising full of faith who will not quit, who will not give up or give in to the lies of the devil. Now is the time! New era!

God's Glory is filling the earth and His Glory is filling the earth through His holy sons and daughters. This filling isn't temporary either. Surely as the Lord God lives, His glory shall fill the earth (Numbers 14:21). This "filling" is being fulfilled

"Now" through God's separated ones, sanctified ones and Holy ones!

Revival is breaking out and there are sons and daughters who are hungry and on fire, wanting Jesus manifested in fullness. They're hungry to experience the Glory of God, intimacy, presence, power, signs, wonders and miracles! Hungry to win millions of souls to Christ and by God's Grace this New Breed will not be denied!

To experience God's Glory and the fulfillment of His destiny and His high call, The Father takes us on a journey of preparation. That journey is called character building or "The Process" of preparation.

We have not arrived and we're still being prepared for more, but in our 30 + year journey of walking with the Lord, He's imparted some major life lessons that we believe will strengthen you to continue to say yes to the High Call! God promises you, if you will stay the course, obey His voice, and never quit, your yes will be so worth it!

Let us begin by sharing with you a little bit of our journey.

My wife and I met at 14, received Jesus Christ as our Lord and Savior at 19, got married at 20, and had four children by the time we were 23. We were ordained to the ministry at 27 and became Senior Pastors at 36; but boy was there many battles, test, trials, hurts, offenses and more along the way and up to recently! Through it all God has shown Himself faithful!

He has truly been ". . . A very present help in trouble" (Psalm 46:1)!

We both grew up with a lot of dysfunction in our lives as many have in our generation.

Because we didn't know Jesus growing up, by the age of 19 we needed a lot of restoration in our lives.

We'll spare you all the details of the teenage years without Jesus, I'm sure you could imagine!

By the age of 19 we were done with the world. We tried most of it and we were still miserable.

In 1988, we received Jesus as our Lord and Savior and we both felt the call of God upon our lives. We could feel God's destiny calling us!

We got married while being baby Christians a year later in 1989 at 20 years of age. We really sensed God calling us not only individually but as a couple!

Over time, our Pastors and other ministers in our church spoke over our lives that we were being called into the ministry. However, at that time, we were just trying to take care of our four kids while still being restored personally from all the "stuff" that happened before we knew Christ. But God called us! So, fast forward to the age of 27 we were ordained as Elders in the church, then a year later to an Associate Pastor!

We were both serving in a leadership capacity helping other people as we were still going through serious trials of our own. Trials in our finances, temptation to move away for a better job, and "people issues" in the church (what we call DRAMA)! God sovereignly kept us from leaving the church a few times.

There was a time when we had "a good reason" to move from California to Texas. We had family in Texas, there was a great ministry there where we were really being fed the word, and all four of our children loved their children/youth ministry. The cost of living was much less and the job opportunities were much better there. In the natural and even in our hearts we were confident that this was the best thing to do. But after counsel with our Pastor, we knew we needed to go pray again.

Our head said, "well we've been faithful in this church about 10 years and we're not leaving in bitterness" so this is a "good" opportunity to move to Texas (some things we call "good" is not always "God").

After prayer and tears (what we call "eating carpet"), the Lord said "No, you're staying." If we had left maybe it would've been "good" but it wouldn't have prepared us for our true "High Calling!"

Some things can be good, but is it God's perfect will for our lives? As we yielded to the Lord in that season to stay planted in the church God had assigned for us, the Lord began to show us the bigger picture. The bigger picture really wasn't about us, but it was about God's Kingdom and His will being established in and through our lives for many others! See our "Yes" as the body of Christ to the Lord Jesus, will produce great Kingdom fruit in the lives of many people. If we would only OBEY!

God began to impress upon our hearts that our assignment was connected to staying planted in this church and that He had a divine mandate for us to fulfill. We had to "die to our desire to move" and say "not our will but your will Father be done." A lot of times we can all say we want to be like Jesus, but when the rubber meets the road, many people want to jump out of the hard places (what we call the fire). In reality to become more like Jesus, we need to "go through" those hard places because that's where we die to self and really let Jesus live through us.

John 12:24-26

"Most assuredly, I say to you, unless a grain of wheat falls into the ground and dies, it remains alone; but if it dies, it produces much grain. He who loves his life will lose it, and he who hates his life in this world will keep it for eternal life. If anyone serves Me, let him follow Me; and where I am, there My servant will be also. If anyone serves Me, him *My* Father will honor."

2 Corinthians 4:11-12

"For we who live are always delivered to death for Jesus' sake, that the life of Jesus also may be manifested in our mortal flesh. So then death is working in us, but life in you."

Each of us have a high calling from the Lord. However, we must be "willing and obedient" to eat the good of that land (calling).

Isaiah 1:19-20

"If you are willing and obedient, You shall eat the good of the land; But if you refuse and rebel, You shall be devoured by the sword; For the mouth of the LORD has spoken."

So again, we had to choose to die to our wants and desires and stay planted in the church God had assigned us to. Moving to Texas wasn't so much the main issue, it was obedience. Would we humble ourselves like Jesus did and become "obedient" to the point of death (to what we wanted and die to our own desires and choose God's perfect will)?

Philippians 2:8

"And being found in appearance as a man, He humbled Himself and became obedient to *the point of death*, even the death of the cross."

Ultimately, we said YES! And you must do the same.

The call of God on your life is real!

Whether called to ministry, family, business, government or any specific assignment. The call and the dream of God is real!

Just like Abraham, Isaac, Jacob, Joseph, Moses, David, Daniel, Jeremiah, Isaiah and others in the Bible, you also have a Supernatural Destiny, Calling and Dream of God to fulfill!

In this "kingdom age" God has sent you to the earth to proclaim the Gospel of Jesus Christ by the power of the Holy Spirit through the specific gifts and talents He has given you. You must "know" by "revelation" that God has called you into that specific assignment. It first needs to bear witness with your spirit and then there needs to be confirmation from true seasoned Godly authority assigned by God to your life.

If you feel confident that you can achieve what's in your heart to do, then your vision is not big enough. Anything God has truly called you to do will be far greater than what "you" can do. God's true calling will require your totally dependence on Him and His Grace!

You must believe God is greater than your weaknesses and if He called you to do this, He will empower you, prepare you, provide for you, protect you and prosper you in this great calling He has on your life!

You're not a wimp, you're a warrior! Rise up in faith and determine that no fear, past failures or future circumstances will stop you from trusting God and believing and obeying the high call, GOD has on your life!

Philippians 4:13

"I can do all things through Christ who strengthens me."

Isaiah 41:10-14 clearly says:

"Fear not, for I *am* with you; Be not dismayed, for I *am* your God. I will strengthen you, Yes, I will help you, I will uphold you with My righteous right hand.'

"Behold, all those who were incensed against you. Shall be ashamed and disgraced; They shall be as nothing, And those who strive with you shall perish. You shall seek them and not find them— Those who contended with you. Those who war against you. Shall be as nothing, As a nonexistent thing. For I, the Lord your God, will hold your right hand, Saying to you, 'Fear not, I will help you. "Fear not, you worm Jacob, You men of Israel! I will help you," says the Lord And your Redeemer, the Holy One of Israel."

God The Almighty is with you, rise up in Him and "be strong in the Lord and in the power of His might" (Ephesians 6:10).

Most of the things we have done in our lives, we were unqualified, unprepared, lacked wisdom and lacked strength or ability; but when we humbled ourselves and trusted in God's Mighty strength, He always strengthened us! He will do the same for you every time you ask but you must believe this. You must believe that God is greater than your weakness and inability. You must believe that greater is Christ in you "than He that is in the world" (1 John 4:4).

Whatever your assignment is in the earth, whether a Pastor, anointed mother, kingdom business person, Psalmist, school teacher, government official, Prophet to the nations, whatever God has called you to fulfill in the earth will require a deep understanding of who you are in Christ. God is more concerned about your "who" rather than your "do." He is more concerned with who you're becoming as a son and daughter and your intimacy and relationship with Him rather than what you're doing, your accomplishments, achievements and successes in the kingdom, etc.

You need to know who you are in Christ first and foremost. We can't stress enough how vitally important it is to personally grow in the revelation of who you are in Christ and "who" you belong to! The revelation that God so loved you personally that He gave His Son to die for you, to save you, heal you, and restore you to Himself must be rooted in the core of your heart. From that revelation you "know" that you "know" that you "know" God loves "you" for who "you" are, not for what you do!

You don't have to earn God's love. You don't have to do everything right, you don't have to perform for God, or do enough good things to be accepted by Him! You are already accepted in the beloved (Jesus).

You believe and know according to God's Word, "Beloved now we are the children of God" (1 John 3:2), because this has everything to do with your security. Spirit, soul and body security. To be honest, it would be very difficult to lead people being insecure yourself. We can't just function, work and pursue the call of God out of our gifts and talents. We must be secure internally. We must be rooted and grounded in the Love of God. If you do not know who you are in Christ and who you belong to, this can cause God's destiny (whatever the destiny may be) for your life to come crumbling down under the pressure of family, ministry, business etc.

The desire to fulfill the destiny of God for your life cannot be driven by insecurity, selfish ambition, pride, jealousy, or to prove oneself. If these impure motives drive you, it can cause you to quit while in the middle of fulfilling your God-given destiny because of pressure; or even cause you to commit major sin or make major ungodly decisions that will destroy not only the work and destiny God has entrusted to you, but potentially destroy your very own life. God Loves you so much and He does not want "you" destroyed for the sake of fulfilling His calling on your life. We must watch and pray! We must be rooted in God's Love and we must be driven by Love!

I Corinthians 16:14

"Let all *that* you *do* be done with love."

Let Love compel your motive to fulfill the call!

2 Corinthians 5:14

"For the love of Christ compels us . . ."

We're no longer living for ourselves, we're living for Christ!

2 Corinthians 5:15

"and He died for all, that those who live should live no longer for themselves, but for Him who died for them and rose again."

The desire to fulfill the call of God must be motivated by love. To be totally transparent that's where the rubber meets the road! Sometimes we might "feel" the love for God, and the love for people, but other times we might not "feel" the love of God. But we don't live by what we "feel." We live by faith" (Romans 1:17) and "faith comes by hearing, and hearing by the word of God" (Romans 10:17). Romans 5:5 says God's love is already in our hearts right now by the Holy Spirit. So whether we "feel" the love of God or not, by faith we "know" based on Romans 5:5, we "have" the love of God in our hearts "Right Now"! But we must ask the Holy Spirit to help us grow in the love of God!!!

Philippians 1:9-11

"And this I pray, that your love may abound still more and more in knowledge and all discernment, that you may approve the things that are excellent, that you may be sincere and without offense till the day of Christ, being filled with the fruits of righteousness which are by Jesus Christ, to the glory and praise of God."

How do we get rooted and grounded in God's Love:

1) **Get scriptures about God's love for you personally.** Read those scriptures. Put those scriptures in your ears, in your eyes and in your heart daily according to Proverbs 4:20-24. Then speak those scriptures out loud to yourself. Speaking the scriptures to yourself is biblical meditation and when you meditate on the word of God it will prosper, restore, and heal your soul.

3 John 2

Beloved, I pray that you may prosper in all things and be in health, just as your soul prospers."

2) **Focus on the love of God for ourselves and for others**. On purpose think about God's love for you and others! Say to yourself "God loves Me" say "God loves you . . . (add your name). Speak to yourself that God loves you. This is very Powerful. Then Go tell someone "God loves you"! Sow love, you'll Reap love!

3) **Passing the Love test!**

Walking out the love of God with people and in various situations is the test itself.

When we yield to the love of God (when we have been hurt or offended by someone) that's when we "truly" get rooted and grounded in Him. It is then and only then that we are conformed to Christ. In the fire of trials, the impurities in us come to the surface and if we yield to the love of God, we will die to ourselves and Christ will live through us. Jesus said surely offenses will come. There will be hurts, disappointments, etc. with people but love never fails. Love always wins!

Reflection Scriptures

Jeremiah 29: 11

"For I know the thoughts that I think toward you, says the LORD. Thoughts of peace and not of evil, to give you a future and a hope."

Isaiah 55:11

"So shall My word be that goes forth from My mouth; It shall not return to Me void, But it shall accomplish what I please, And it shall proper *in the thing* for which I sent it."

Job 23: 14

"For He performs *what is* appointed for me, And many such *things are* with Him."

Psalm 138:8

The Lord will perfect *that which* concerns me; Your mercy, O LORD, *endures* forever; Do not forsake the works of Your hands."

Ephesians 2:10

"For we are His workmanship, created in Christ Jesus for good works, which God prepared beforehand that we should walk in them."

Philippians 1:6

"being confident of this very thing, that He who has begun a good work in you will complete *it* until the day of Jesus Christ;"

Let us pray for you

Father we pray that you would strengthen every reader and every one of us to say with a pure heart "not our will but your will Father be done." Strengthen us to die to our own desires and "Obey" your high calling upon our lives in Jesus' Name! Amen.

CHAPTER II
SEASONING AND MATURITY THROUGH THE FIRE

Mark 9:49-50

"For everyone will be seasoned with fire, and every sacrifice will be seasoned with salt. Salt *is* good, but if the salt loses its flavor, how will you season it? Have salt in yourselves, and have peace with one another."

Jesus said everyone will be seasoned with fire. And every sacrifice will be seasoned with salt.

When you say yes to the call of God, there is joy to do His will. He gives us the desire to do His will. He anoints your eyes to see the destiny, the calling, and the great plan He is directing you to fulfill.

To prepare you for this great calling however, there will be a seasoning with the fire of the Holy Spirit in your life. The greater the calling, the deeper the preparation. We know this principle even in secular careers. If you want a job changing tires or doing oil changes then you have to go apply, get trained and start working. If you want to become a doctor however or a lawyer, there will be years of preparation required.

The greater the responsibility, the greater the preparation. The greater the calling, the deeper the internal preparation of our character will be.

The fire of God purifies us, kills the carnal nature, and prepares us to serve our generation with a clean heart. God's destiny is powerful! God's destiny has fulfillment and purpose! It has potential to leave a powerful legacy that your very life pushes forth the Gospel of Jesus Christ to your generation.

Your life impacts the earth for the Glory of God. Millions of souls have been eternally saved and changed by God's Grace and because you said "yes." God's destiny is much greater than your life's plan. But to step into that destiny and to fulfill that destiny we must say "yes" to the fire of the Holy Spirit!

Take up your cross and follow Jesus.

Matthew 16:24

"Then Jesus said to His disciples, "If anyone desires to come after Me, let him deny himself, and take up his cross, and follow Me."

It's a fantasy that everything's going to go smooth ALL the time. There will be resistance when you're doing God's will and pressing into the kingdom of God, just like there was in the Apostle Paul's day when the Holy Spirit directed Him to go preach the gospel in certain places. So also the other Apostles and disciples. But God is faithful!

Are we willing to partake of the sufferings of Christ? The call of discipleship is a call "to know Him and to make Him known." Our ministry, as God's holy sons and daughters, is one of separation to The Lord and a pure heart towards God and people. So in reality, to partake of the glory of God, we must also partake of His sufferings. Ultimately, we must die to the selfish part of us.

Philippians 1:6

"being confident of this very thing, that He who has begun a good work in you will complete *it* until the day of Jesus Christ."

Knowing we are called to the ministry, we NEED to go through the process of many tests and trials in relationships and other areas to be ready for what entails ministry. The test of love is the majority of the process. God is going to purify our motives in every area of our life. Knowing "who we are" in Christ as a son and daughter in Him and being rooted and grounded in His love, is the absolute foundation for every child of God to overcome the many trials of life. Circumstances in life happens, so therefore our trust "must" be FULLY in the Lord and grounded in His love to overcome them.

We have been through many personal trials and fires. The fiery trial we shared in Chapter I, concerning whether we were to stay at the church God assigned us to, or leave that church required us to lay down our own desire for the sake of God's calling. We both agreed that the Lord was leading us to stay. So with many tears we yielded to the Holy Spirit as He began to burn out our own plans and desires until we said yes Lord! There were many tears but in the end we yielded to the Holy Spirit and the love of God. We remained in our church and eventually became the Senior Pastors and Apostolic Overseers of this same church! To God be the glory forever!

That was one of our fires, was it easy? No. Was it worth it? Yes.

Your fiery trial will not be easy but just like Joseph, Daniel and the three Hebrew boys you will come out of your fire, be promoted in the Kingdom of God and be used by God to bring deliverance to many people in need of the saving grace of God!

Reflection Scriptures

Isaiah 48:10

"Behold, I have refined you, but not as silver; I have tested you in the furnace of affliction."

Isaiah 43:2

"When you pass through the waters, I *will* be with you; And through the rivers, they shall not overflow you. When you walk through the fire, you shall not be burned, Nor shall the flame scorch you."

Isaiah 41:10

"Fear not, for I *am* with you; Be not dismayed, for I *am* your God. I will strengthen you, Yes, I will help you, I will uphold you with My righteous right hand."

Job 13:15

"Though He slay me, yet will I trust Him. . ."

Job 23:10

"But He knows the way that I take; *When* He has tested me, I shall come forth as gold."

1 Peter 5:10

"But may the God of all grace, who called us to His eternal glory by Christ Jesus, after you have suffered a while, perfect, establish, strengthen, and settle you."

Let us pray for you

Father I pray in Jesus' name that you would strengthen every person reading this with your grace to say "yes" to your perfect will! Let them see the joy that is set before them. Give them not only the courage, the love, and the ability to say "Yes" and never quit, but to go through the fire and to know by revelation that You are with them and will never leave them! I declare that this person reading and praying with us right now, shall fulfill your High Calling Father, in the name of Jesus. Be Blessed now with God's power to go through "the fire" and fulfill His will in Jesus' name! Amen.

CHAPTER III
INTEGRITY

Definition of Integrity:

1. Wholeness; entireness; unbroken state.

2. The entire, unimpaired state of anything, particularly of the mind; moral soundness or purity; incorruptness; uprightness; honesty. *integrity* comprehends the whole moral character, but has a special reference to uprightness in mutual dealings, transfers of property, and agencies for others.

3. Purity; genuine, unadulterated, unimpaired state; as the *integrity* of language.

In·teg·ri·ty

noun

1. the quality of being honest and having strong moral principles; moral uprightness.

At times it seems the word integrity is a foreign word in our society. It's one thing to know what integrity is, but it's another thing to know how integrity affects our lives, our families, our relationships and our society. It's also another thing to "commit daily" to living a life of integrity.

We all fall short of God's glory at different times in our lives, we all make mistakes and we are constantly growing to become more Christ like. However, every one of us must have a zero tolerance for a lack of integrity. What's unfortunate is sometimes as leaders we place a higher demand on the people we are leading then we do ourselves. We want them to be responsible, to communicate with a right attitude, to keep their word, to be loyal and trustworthy while we fail to consistently do the same. As servant leaders we must understand that to whom much is given much is required (Luke 12:48).

If you are a parent, you are a leader in the family. If you are a pastor, you are a leader in the church. If you are a business owner, you are a leader in your business. Whatever form of leadership you have, without integrity your life and your words cannot be trusted.

Without trust, relationships will be weak and even broken. Without a solid relationship with others, destinies can't be fulfilled.

God will bring other people into your life to help you fulfill His purpose and your destiny. But you must have integrity in those relationships. Remember, if you do not have integrity, your relationships will be undermined, weak and even potentially broken. No matter how hard or long you work, no matter how much you pray, fast and read the Bible, live on fire for God, win souls, have great miracles and have fire to fulfill God's destiny, nothing can make up for not having integrity in relationships.

In fact, if you do not have strong godly relationships, God's destiny will not come to pass! You need faithful kingdom relationships to fulfill God's destiny. However, if you consistently have a lack of integrity in your life, you will destroy those kingdom relationships that God gave you to fulfill His calling and destiny.

A lack of communication in relationships can destroy our integrity as leaders. When we've done our best to communicate with a person if we absolutely couldn't keep an appointment for a call or a meeting and to reschedule that meeting to have integrity on our side of things, and the other person doesn't, it's damaging. Often times we have experienced people that are leaders in churches or in ministry that say they are going to contact us at a specific time or day for an important conversation who didn't.

In these situations, they didn't hold to their word, and they didn't communicate with us at all! As a result, we became disappointed. Disappointed because we actually put our time aside to wait for that scheduled appointment with them. Knowing these were leaders or friends of ours, caused frustration in the relationship.

God Has Integrity, We Must Have Integrity

We must have integrity because our Father God has integrity. He does not go back on His word. Therefore, we trust God because he has given us His eternal word and He does not break it.

Psalms 89:34-35

"My covenant I will not break, Nor alter the word that has gone out of My lips. Once I have sworn by My holiness; I will not lie to David."

Numbers 23:19

"God is not a man, that He should lie, Nor a son of man, that He should repent. Has He said, and will He not do? Or has He spoken, and will He not make it good?"

God is love and love speaks truly, deals truly, keeps truth at all cost!

Ephesians 5:1-2

We are to be "imitators of God as dear children. And walk in Love . . ."

I John 4:8

"He who does not love does not know God, for God is love."

We MUST, Change the Tide!

When parents love their children, they will do their best to keep their promises to their children. If a parent always tells the child they will do something but they never do it, the children will no longer "trust" the words of the parent and eventually begin to be disappointed with the parent, disrespect the parent and withdraw from having a strong relationship with the parent.

This same scenario happens far too often in many areas of society. As leaders we must change the course and change the tide where there's a flood of "the lack of integrity."

It's time that we raise the standard by putting a strong demand on ourselves to walk daily in integrity.

INTEGRITY, INTEGRITY, INTEGRITY!

Let's keep saying it, living it and being an example of it until the next generation (youth) knows that integrity is normal and having a lack of integrity is weird (abnormal and sin).

Marriages, families, churches, businesses, governmental leaders and governmental systems have all been shaken or destroyed because of "lack of integrity."

Some of our greatest leaders and institutions have been shaken, weakened, and even destroyed because of this underlying "fault line" of a lack of integrity. Earthquakes cause great damage which all starts at a fault line. Shaking in our lives and society can cause great damage if we lack this powerful force called INTEGRITY!

We must awaken as leaders and recognize on our watch, this avalanche of "the downfall of integrity" is happening! Let's arise on the strength of God's grace and raise the standard of integrity in this generation.

Integrity is strong,

lack of integrity is weak.

Integrity builds nations,

lack of integrity destroys nations.

Integrity breeds healthy societies,

lack of integrity breeds sick societies.

Integrity blesses the next generation,

lack of integrity can destroy the next generation.

Proverbs 20:7

Integrity is godly,

lack of integrity is ungodly.

Integrity is Jesus style,

lack of integrity is the devil's style.

Integrity breeds success,

lack of integrity breeds failure.

Integrity strengthens relationships,

lack of integrity weakens and destroys relationships.

Integrity is a bridge to life,

lack of integrity is a bridge to death.

Integrity is a key character trait to fulfilling your destiny,

lack of integrity undermines and limits the fulfillment of your destiny.

Develop Integrity! It's worth it! God is Honored! God is Glorified! You gain respect, honor and favor. It's time the current tide of a lack of integrity is turned and a new generation arises full of the power of Christ and this powerful Christ like attribute called integrity! Let's do this!

Reflection Scriptures

Proverbs 10:9

"He who walks with integrity walks securely, But he who perverts his ways will become known."

A king (Governmental Leader) said!

Genesis 20:5

"Did he not say to me, 'She *is* my sister'? And she, even she herself said, 'He *is* my brother.' In the integrity of my heart and innocence of my hands I have done this."

God's Response to the King!

Genesis 20:6

And God said to him in a dream, "Yes, I know that you did this in the integrity of your heart. For I also withheld you from sinning against Me; therefore I did not let you touch her."

1 King 9:4

"Now if you walk before Me as your father David walked, in integrity of heart and in uprightness, to do according to all that I have commanded you, *and* if you keep My statutes and My judgments ..."

Job 2:3

"Then the Lord said to Satan, "Have you considered My servant Job, that *there is* none like him on the earth, a blameless and upright man, one who fears God and shuns evil? And still he holds fast to his integrity, although you incited Me against him, to destroy him without cause.""

Job 2:9

"Then his wife said to him, "Do you still hold fast to your integrity? Curse God and die!""

Job 27:5

"Far be it from me that I should say you are right; Till I die I will not put away my integrity from me."

Job 31:6

"Let me be weighed on honest scales, that God may know my integrity."

Psalm 78:72

"So he shepherded them according to the integrity of his heart, And guided them by the skillfulness of his hands."

Proverbs 11:3

"The integrity of the upright will guide them, But the perversity of the unfaithful will destroy them."

Proverbs 19:1

"Better *is* the poor who walks in his integrity than *one who is* perverse in his lips, and is a fool."

Proverbs 20:7

"The righteous *man* walks in his integrity; His children *are* blessed after him."

Proverbs 28:6

"Better *is* the poor who walks in his integrity Than one perverse *in his* ways, though he *be* rich."

Titus 2:7

". . . in all things showing yourself *to be* a pattern of good works; in doctrine *showing* integrity, reverence, incorruptibility . . ."

Let us pray for you

Father we pray for everyone reading this book, and we ask you to strengthen conviction, wisdom, and grace to walk daily in integrity! We pray that your love Heavenly Father would motivate them to keep their word even when it hurts. We pray Father that you would destroy the tide of the lack of integrity in the Kingdom of God, in our nation and around the world. Let the spirit of Integrity be released from heaven into the hearts of every reader and bear fruit in their lives, families and society. Let a new generation ARISE, starting with all of us individually, who will commit to living and growing daily in true godly integrity. According Mark 11:24 We Believe we receive all this in Jesus' Name! Amen.

CHAPTER IV
HUMILITY

God will pass over 10,000 gifted people to find one humble person!

A person that has few gifts, but great humility before God, will be empowered by the mighty grace of God to fulfill God's destiny.

Maybe you don't feel qualified to do something great for the Lord. Guess what? You're the right candidate God is looking for because he will choose the weak things of the world to confound the wise! God chooses the base things, the things that are not in order to put to shame the things that are (1Corinthians 1:26-29).

I was born in South Central L.A., to a handicapped single mother. My mother had a major car accident as a teenager where she flew through the front windshield of her father's car. By God's Grace and much prayer, she had a partial recovery. However, due to her handicap she was not able to raise me as a little boy. I have never known my dad. I lived with several aunts when I was really young. However, most of my upbringing was by my mother's sister and her husband.

God, by His grace, saved me in May of 1988 at the age of 19. There I was searching for love, identity and purpose and God rescued me! What a good, good God! I had nothing to offer God, no skills, no great abilities, no natural father, not living with my mom, no money, no future. But God said I love you and I have a purpose for your life. Now that's Grace! He'll do the same and even greater for you! I had to humble myself, surrender my life and follow Jesus! That was the greatest decision of my life!

If you will humble yourself, surrender your life and follow Jesus, He will do greater things in your life than you can ever imagine! God can and will anoint a man who will humble himself and obey His voice! Humility comes before honor, promotion and riches.

Proverbs 18:12

"Before destruction the heart of a man is haughty, And before honor *is* humility."

Proverbs 22:4

"By humility *and* the fear of the Lord *Are* riches and honor and life."

Deuteronomy 8:2-3

"And you shall remember that the LORD your God led you all the way these forty years in the wilderness, to humble you and test you, to know what *was* in your heart, whether you would keep His commandments or not. So He humbled you, allowed you to hunger, and fed you with manna which you did not know nor did your fathers know, that He might make you know that man shall not live by bread alone; but man lives by every *word* that proceeds from the mouth of the LORD."

Humility is a MUST and prerequisite to the fivefold ministry and in any form of true leadership. When you are leading people as a senior leader or lay leader in the church or business, you don't have the right to react to those who have been entrusted in your care to disciple. We as leaders have more accountability (biblically speaking), to walk humbly and not react in the flesh when those we are trying to help react wrongfully to us.

There are many lives that need restoration and they don't know how to receive instruction from a leader in their lives yet. When this happens, we've learned we can't take it personal! We must keep our hearts soft before God and have a serving perspective. According to Matthew 23:11, the greatest in the kingdom will be a servant of all.

We knew we were called to the ministry in a wider capacity, but we had a process of maturing in Christ first! Even though we knew this call was real and God had confirmed it many times, we had to be content in our season when we were raising four children. My husband had a full time job and I was home taking care of the children and our home. We both were also involved with several "help" ministries in the church. We loved God and wanted to be faithful but it wasn't easy. We went through several difficult financial ups and downs through those years and "people trials" (even in the church) which was very stressful while raising a large family, but God!

We didn't RUN from the hurdles of life, we learned FROM them! We chose to yield to the Lord and we could sense the Holy Spirit continually drawing us closer to Him! Thank you Jesus! With conviction, the Holy fear of the Lord in our hearts to keep seeking Him, years went by and seasons came and went, but we kept moving forward in our relationship with the Lord! Why? Not because of ministry but because we knew that we needed Him more than ever and without Him, we are nothing!

When you have a close relationship with the Lord, you will feel the conviction and the need to walk humbly unto the Lord, but also towards people, even to your own hurt at times. That is a big part of the maturing process of "Christ likeness" and in passing many "humility tests." This also helps us grow up in Gods unconditional love, "that Christ may dwell in your hearts through faith; that you, being rooted and grounded in love" (Ephesians 3:17).

According to Matthew 5:9 "Blessed *are* the peacemakers, For they will be called children of God." I can't stress how vital it is to have a clean conscious towards God and to go and initiate peace with someone who was obvious in the wrong; and to humble ourselves and be at peace with that person no matter who is right or wrong.

The key is humbling ourselves and not having to be right! If a person is willing to talk something through in a humble matter, that can be a fruitful resolve in a situation, no matter how sticky the situation may be. On the other hand, if one is not humble, then there won't be fruit. But isn't that what we should always want as Gods child and servant of the Lord? To be fruitful? If not, what are we doing? What are we after? What should be the condition of our hearts?

Remember, Jesus never reviled back when He was reviled, nor did He open His mouth to defend Himself. Because of this, we should always strive for reconciliation! For the Holy Spirit is the Spirit of reconciliation. This is the fruit of the love of our Lord, Humility!

Humility is an attribute of purity! The Word of God says, "Blessed *are* the pure in heart! For they shall see God" (Matthew 5:8). God requires humility as the first step to heal and revive a land, a nation, a people! Humility is required of us all.

Reflection Scriptures

2 Chronicles 7:14

"If My people who are called by My name will humble themselves, and pray and seek My face, and turn from their wicked ways, then I will hear from heaven, and will forgive their sin and heal their land."

Humility is one of the 3 Major moral attributes that God requires of mankind!

Micah 6:8

"He has shown you, O man, what *is* good; And what does the LORD require of you But to do justly, To love mercy, And to walk humbly with your God?"

Isaiah 57:15

"For thus says the High and Lofty One who inhabits eternity, whose name is Holy: "I dwell in the high and holy *place*, With him *who* has a contrite and humble spirit, To revive the spirit of the humble, And to revive the heart of the contrite ones."

Isaiah 66:2 KJV

"For all those things mine My hand made, and all those things have been, saith the LORD: but to this man will I look, even to him that is poor and of a contrite spirit, and trembleth at my word."

Proverbs 29:23

"A man's pride will bring him low, But the humble in spirit will retain honor."

1 Peter 5:6

"Therefore humble yourselves under the mighty hand of God, that He may exalt you in due time . . ."

Matthew 20:26

"Yet it shall not be so among you; but whoever desires to become great among you, let him be your servant."

Let us prayer for you

Father we pray for those reading this right now, strengthen each one by your Holy Spirit to grow in humility. Father I thank you that those who are born again through faith in Jesus Christ have your divine nature on the inside of them (2 Peter 1:3). Help them today Father to live crucified with Christ, dead to pride, and by faith to walk in humility. To submit to you Father and resist the devil and he will flee from them. Father you said you give grace to the humble. Let the fruit of the Holy Spirit and this beautiful Christ like attribute of humility grow every day in their lives. In Jesus' Name Amen!

CHAPTER V
LEAD WHILE YOU BLEED

When we were going through many different trials we had to make a decision to keep moving forward! Our Pastor trained us to continue to put one foot in front of the other and never quit! In fact, before he went to heaven to be with the Lord he said don't quit, keep moving and don't compromise!

We remember having to continue to lead, serve and give to others after our Pastor got sick and went to be with the Lord suddenly. Before our Pastor got sick, the church was in a good place. We were Associate Pastors and the church was birthing new projects. We were preparing to do prison ministry. Many young adults were on fire and wanting to reach souls for Christ!

In the midst of this momentum, we noticed our Pastor was getting skinnier and skinnier. Tragically, eight months later he passed away from cancer. At that time most of us in the church were hurting, disappointed and discouraged.

Before passing, our Pastor asked us, his Associate Pastors, to take up the church and be the Senior Pastors. Before his request we never wanted to be Senior Pastors, especially with a grieving church. Nevertheless, we became Senior Pastors.

After we became Senior Pastors, there were people who stood with us and pledged to stand with us to fulfill the vision God had given our church. Some gave us swords, letters, framed letter commitments that they would stay with us. Many of those people left! People leaving the Church hurt us a lot, but we had to continue to lead while bleeding.

There was a time, about 2 years after becoming Senior Pastor, that we absolutely felt like quitting. We had 4 teenagers and we were still new at being Senior Pastors. Our children were all growing up and growing in their identity, but they were being tempted to do things they knew better not to do.

We cried more than ever that year. We felt very discouraged because of all the trials in our family and in the church.

There were problems in our family, problems in the Eldership of the church, problems with church members and we were going through trials in our finances. There was not much income coming in the church to even cover all the church's monthly budget.

This *was* an opportunity to quit!

At times we felt like "why are we even doing this"! Should we continue or quit? I remember one night after a major trial with my daughter, being on my knees next to the bed and crying my eyes out. I wanted to quit. Thinking in my mind "I didn't sign up for all this!"

For us, through our personal experience, we continued to give out, in spite of what we felt. We learned even if you've been hurt or betrayed, lead while you bleed!

Isaiah 58:6-12 says you will be healed as you serve other

Proverbs 11:25

Water and you will be watered.

Give and you will receive (Luke 6:38).

These are Kingdom principles. When you're walking in your assignment fulfilling God's purpose for your life, there will be enemies on the call of God, evil forces will try to stop God's destiny for your life!

Like Jesus, there will be disappointments, betrayals and hurts, but by the grace of God we must choose to continue to serve others and minister to others even in our restoration process.

Your sacrifice will have reward. What you do in secret, God will reward you openly (Matthew 6:4).

Your pain will give life, strength and victory to others!

LEAD WHILE YOU BLEED!

Keys to Lead While You Bleed:

1. Abiding in God's Presence.

We're all busy but being in God's Presence DAILY is an absolute must if we are going to continue to lead, serve and fulfill our destiny!

Whatever your assignment on earth is, hell wants to stop you from fulfilling God's assignment. Whether a doctor, government official, preacher, etc.

You will need a daily, fresh infilling of His presence, grace, wisdom, love, peace and much more that comes from his glorious presence in order to finish the race!

2. Take it one day at a time!

Daily ask the Lord for an abundance of grace and peace to fill your heart and mind!

3. Maintaining a repentant and surrendered heart- Huge!!!

Be quick to repent! Don't make excuses, just confess, turn from that sinful thing and go on!

4. Guarding your hearts diligently!

If we're going to finish right, a pure heart is an absolute necessity.

Blessed are the pure in heart for they shall see God (Matthew 5:8 KJV)!

5. Allow the Lord to cut and divide soul and spirit (purifying our motives).

6. Humility

We can't stress enough the importance of humility!

Brokenness has been so vital and a major key to the restoration process in our lives!

Through the many battles we had to choose to humble ourselves and not give in to pride, bitterness and anger. When we had the many opportunities to become prideful, by the grace of God we chose humility instead!

We all have to choose to get better and not bitter.

". . . A broken spirit and a contrite heart these- oh God you will not despise" (Psalm 51:17).

7. Focus your mind on the things above.

Guard your thoughts!

It's important not to think about the hurts, ask why or over analyze the situation because that can reopen the wound and cause your healing process to take longer!

When choosing to go forward, even while hurting, the Lord may say, "put this situation on the altar, commit the people to God and move forward." Keep loving God, loving people and make the devil eat dirt by fulfilling your destiny!

8. Keep the vision burning in your heart!

What God said is true! His prophetic promises will strengthen you!

9. Wisdom of Heaven!

Ask God who to talk to and who not to talk to. We learned this ourselves through trial and error.

There were times when we reached out to people to get wisdom, counsel or understanding to make sure we were discerning a problem correctly. While sometimes the counsel we received was good and fruitful, however there were times when our private information became public. This occurred simply because we lacked wisdom by trusting people who were anointed and gifted but lacked the godly character to be trusted with the private matters of our heart!

Please use wisdom with who you share the private matters of your heart with!

10. Know your body clock

Get the proper rest you need. Hurts and negative things can run through your mind when you're tired. Frustration, anger and disappointments can bring more discouragement when you don't have enough rest.

11. Endurance!!!

You have need for endurance!

David was hurting but he had to encourage himself in the Lord!

He went into prayer and got a Word from the Father who said pursue, overtake and recover all!

Granted there are real situations. If someone went through a traumatic situation they might need to take time off from ministry to be healed and restored. However, in our situation and in many situations like King David, like Paul, like Jesus, by the GRACE OF GOD, we continued to lead while bleeding!

Be thankful and look at the people who are being faithful, bearing fruit and changing!

Reflection Scriptures

Isaiah 40:29

He gives power to the weak, And to *those who* have no might He increases strength."

Jeremiah 17:14

"Heal me, O Lord, and I shall be healed; Save me and I shall be saved, for you are my praise."

Psalm 6:2

"Have mercy on me, O Lord, for I am weak; O Lord, heal me, for my bones are troubled."

Psalm 147:3

"He heals the brokenhearted And binds up their wounds."

Psalm 119:28

"My soul melts from heaviness; Strengthen me according to Your word."

Philippians 4:13

"I can do all things through Christ which strengthens me."

Let us pray for you

Father I thank you for those that are leading now and those who You are preparing to lead in this generation. Strengthen them to continue to lead even when it hurts! Strengthen them with your mighty grace Father to keep moving, never quit, and never compromise. Lord Jesus you said your grace is sufficient, when they are weak you are strong! You said they that wait on the Lord shall renew their strength, they will mount up with wings as eagles. They will run and not grow weary they will walk and not faint! As they wait on you, trust in you, and keep moving forward to obey your great kingdom assignment you have in their lives, Father we ask for fresh power from your throne of grace to come to them every day. In Jesus' Name. Amen

CHAPTER VI
LOVE

I t's for our good that we actually go through very difficult situations. It's a type of suffering in Christ. If anything, when we go through tests (that's the key, go through), we become more conformed to Christ. But there's a flip side, when we do not go through tests there is no growth.

Had we not gone through our various tests we would not have grown and matured in the love of God! We would've stayed at the same level that we were at. By going through our tests, we've learned the major key to surviving being tested is love!

Love when it hurts. It always wins! Really!

By going through the fire (tests) we have proven that love always wins, love never fails and love always comes out on top!

Really! We've had to walk through this many times. We are living testimonies that it really works, even when it really hurts! Choosing to walk in love is the only way to live and enjoy life on earth and there is no greater love than to lay down our lives for others!

God is love and love never quits! Love believes all things, hopes all things, endures all things. Love never fails!

If you're still reading this book, there's something in you that says I want to honor God, love God and obey God's high calling on my life!

There's something in you that is calling you to a deeper place in God! Something saying I will not settle for second-best. I will love God, I will know God, walk with God and fulfill my purpose in God. Because this is you, you're a part of this great remnant on earth right now determined to see the glory of God fill the earth.

However, in your journey, your love walk will be tested. All of us will go through the love test. Educated, uneducated, Black, White, Hispanic, Asian, rich, poor, successful, or unsuccessful, you will be offended at some point. There will be hurts, disappointments and situations that will try to poison your heart to carry things that the human heart was never created to carry.

The human heart was created to have love, peace, happiness, hope, faith and joy; but if we let hate, unforgiveness and bitterness remain in our hearts these things will become like poison. Let it go and walk in love!

We've gone through many love test in our lives! When we started with our international ministry, our love walk was really tested. Our family went through many spiritual battles after we started traveling abroad. There were many hurts and disappointments. Some things we never thought we would go through, well we went through it!

One time while we were in another nation ministering and experiencing the power of God, we got a really disturbing message. A major sin was taking place in the church. We were totally shocked! We will not go into the details because love covers a multitude of sins, but we will tell you this story because it was very disappointing and it hurt others as well as our hearts; we were upset!

While God was using us to minister to many people in Brazil, there were assignments of the devil trying to distract our hearts and stop us from doing the work God had called us to do. In that situation we had to choose to love and forgive even though our flesh wanted to react and not love. We had to make a decision to humble our hearts and forgive.

Moments like these are hurtful. When the devil is trying to distract you he's not going to always use people that you don't know. He will try to use people that you love dearly and are close to you so that it can affect you. Sometimes it might be your immediate family, good friends, church leaders, etc. but like Jesus, we have to make a decision and commit to the love walk at all times. We had to choose to get better and not get bitter!

The Bible says guard your heart with all diligence, for out of the heart are the "forces" of life (Proverbs 4:23). Just like the natural heart is the most important organ of the body, so is our spiritual heart to our entire life. We must guard and protect our hearts from unforgiveness, bitterness, pride, anger, etc. Remember, we are not fighting against flesh and blood but against principalities and powers in the heavenly places. This is a good fight of faith.

Even when we don't feel like forgiving and walking in love, we choose to believe the love of God is already in our hearts by the Holy Spirit, according to Romans 5:5. When we choose to walk in that love no matter what we feel; love will always win. Love will always give you victory. Love is God and God is love.

God cannot be defeated and love cannot be defeated. You will win! You will fulfill your destiny! You will be an unstoppable force in this generation if you will guard your heart, be humble and walk in love! This is the only way to truly be conformed to Christ!!!!

GOD BLESSES WHAT YOU SAY AND GOD BLESSES WHAT YOU DON'T SAY!

There's so many times we could have said things in the heat of the battle!

Just because it's right to say something, doesn't mean it's right according to love!

Sometimes love will stop your tongue from saying something to someone even though you're right and they're wrong; or maybe we're wrong and they're right and the Lord is correcting you through someone He has put in your life to help you. Even then love won't react but respond in humility! These are the tests that we must pass to be rooted and grounded in God's love (Ephesians 3:17)!

Love will choose to be "slow to speak, quick to hear and slow to anger" (James 1:19)!

Wow that is such great wisdom!

In our marriage, that has been such a great key! At the time of writing this book we've been married 30 years (Thank you Jesus)! Being slow to speak, quick to hear and slow to anger has HELPED us avoid many disagreements, conflicts and moments of regret. But only when we "choose" to walk in love, when we "choose" to be slow to speak, quick to hear and slow to anger!

There's been times in our marriage when we were trying to talk through a situation and we just didn't agree. We each had our opinion of what was right but we had to "choose" love! We had to "choose" to be slow to speak and listen to what one another was really saying, and not to get angry if we didn't understand or agree. We came to realize that we both wanted the same thing but we had a different edge on it!

Now if we chose to argue, to prove our point, be quick to speak, slow to hear, and quick to anger, (which can happen and does happen in many marriages) that would become a recipe for destruction! That's not love, that's pride! Pride comes before destruction and a haughty spirit before a fall (Proverbs 16:18). Jesus has helped us in our marriage all these years and He's still helping us daily! That's where the mighty grace of God comes in. Jesus by His grace helps us to walk in love, helps us to be slow to speak, quick to hear and slow to anger. We need the mighty Holy Spirit (who is the Spirit of Jesus in us) active in our lives and in our marriage to help us daily!

You might feel like "You didn't sign up for all this in your marriage", but remember God's love in us always conquers! Love never fails in our lives and marriages.

Over and over in our journey with Christ, we will have opportunities with family, friends, church family, co-workers, etc. to just speak our mind or what we feel, but love will say, "hold", don't do it! Sometimes the result you want comes on the path of what is very uncomfortable: loving others, dying to self, being humble, "choosing" to do what God's word instructs us to do!

Love doesn't seek its own interest butlLove is seeking for what is best for other people. Love wants to bless people, lift people, heal and help people!

Sometimes those people that we want to love, bless, lift, heal and help, are the very ones who have hurt us! Maybe you were hurt by a family member and you have forgiven them, but you would rather not talk with them or rather not be around them because of how they hurt you. In situations like this, we MUST go to Jesus. When we go to Jesus and give Him our pain, our hurt and our wounds, then Jesus will help us and heal us! Then we need to pray for and bless those who have hurt us and be open if the Lord would have us to reach out to them, show acts of kindness to them, or to do something good for them.

By doing this we demonstrate not human love but God's love in us, which supersedes what we feel! Jesus even said, "love your enemies." Even though that family member or person might not be an enemy, we still need to "love even when it hurts!" Why?!? Because you have been made in the image of God with powerful gifts and talents; you have the grace of Jesus Christ, the power of the Holy Spirit that is ready to explode in this generation and change the world. In your journey to fulfilling your destiny, there will be hurts and trials, but you must commit to the love walk.

Reflection Scriptures

Ephesians 5:2

"And walk in love, as Christ also has loved us and given Himself for us, an offering and a sacrifice to God for a sweet-smelling aroma."

John 13:34

"A new commandment I give to you, that you love one another; as I have loved you, that you also love one another."

John 13:35

"By this all will know that you are My disciples, if you have love for one another."

1 John 4:7

"Beloved, let us love one another, for love is of God; and everyone who loves is born of God and knows God."

1 Peter 2:17

"Honor all *people*. Love the brotherhood. Fear God. Honor the king."

Let us pray for you

Father we Thank you that you are Love and you live on the inside of every born again child of God reading this book. We ask that you would strengthen each reader to know by revelation how much you love them Father God. That they are fully persuaded and know the depth, height, length, and width of your love Father in Jesus' Name (Ephesians 3:14-21). Father as they understand your love for them, strengthen each person to walk in your love, to demonstrate your love and to Increase in your love! (Thessalonians 3:12-13). Let the Fruit of the Spirit GROW in their lives everyday Father. That the world knows we are your disciple because of our love for each other (John 13;35) In Jesus' Name! Amen!

CHAPTER VII
DON'T QUIT YOUR
PAIN HAS GREAT GAIN!

Don't quit God's destiny is real!

Don't quit your destiny will be fulfilled!

Jesus didn't suffer for His own gain, or His own self, He did it for us! He laid down His life for us!

Two years after we started Pastoring I was ready to quit! There was pressure in the family, pressure in finances, pressures in the ministry. It seemed like there were multiple warheads being shot at us all at one time. In my heart I was like, "Lord I didn't sign up for all this! All I wanted to do was obey Jesus, love people and win lost souls for Jesus! But somehow it seemed to start off like WW3 in the spirit (that's what it felt like to me😄).

Well in my soul I was ready to quit. The first few years we cried more than we ever cried before. Just the pain of the trials, the family pressures, the disappointments with people, all that and more seemed to be more than enough to wave the white flag and say, "I'm done, I quit!" We believed God had a big plan, but we didn't know that God's big plan would trigger "all this drama."

My wife and I again decided there's one place God has never failed to meet us. He has always shown up, come through and given us peace in our hearts and mind! We got on our knees and began to cry out to God!

We prayed, and kept praying, and kept praying! God's love truly compelled us! His grace gave us the strength to continue. God, by His grace, gave us the faith to believe that "this too will pass" and we will see the promise that He prophesied over our lives come into manifestation! Well, God showed up, we kept going and today we are walking in the actual manifestation of "some" of the mighty things God has prophesied over our lives, over 20 years ago!

Galatians 6:9

You will not grow weary in well doing, for in due season you will reap because you will not lose heart!

We declare that over your life in Jesus Name!!!

Be strong, be courageous. God is with you and He will not fail you!

Wage war with the prophetic words that have been spoken over your life (1 Timothy 1:18)!

What God has spoken over your life, every prophetic word God has given you, we declare "ALL" shall come to pass!

We release our faith with yours, and believe God to give you grace (favor and blessing), wisdom, strength, peace and power to fulfill the destiny God has for your life!

Father we declare that the word that you have spoken over this one's life will come to pass in Jesus' name!

Father what you have ordained before they were born, we declare your word shall come to pass in Jesus' name!

God said:

Psalm 89:34

"My covenant I will not break, Nor alter the word that has gone out of My lips."

Isaiah 55:8-13

"For My thoughts are not your thoughts, Nor are your ways My ways," says the LORD. "For as the heavens are higher than the earth, So are My ways higher than your ways, And My thoughts than your thoughts. "For as the rain comes down, and the snow from heaven, And do not return there, But water the earth, And make it bring forth and bud, That it may give seed to the sower And bread to the eater, So shall My word be that goes forth from My mouth; It shall not return to Me void, But it shall accomplish what I please, And it shall prosper *in the thing* for which I sent it. "For you shall go out with joy, And be led out with peace; The mountains and the hills Shall break forth into singing before you, And all the trees of the field shall clap their hands. Instead of the thorn shall come up the cypress tree, And instead of the brier shall come up the myrtle tree; And it shall be to the LORD for a name, For an everlasting sign that *shall* not be cut off."

Numbers 23:19-20

"God is not a man, that He should lie, Nor a son of man, that He should repent. Has He said, and will He not do? Or has He spoken, and will He not make it good? Behold, I have received a *command* to bless; He has blessed, and I cannot reverse it."

Believe God! Obey His Word! Fulfill your Destiny!

Before you were born God knew you and ordained your life (Jeremiah 1:5)!

God said I know the plans I have for you . . .

(Jeremiah 29:11).

Faithful is He that called you and He will bring it to pass (1 Thessalonians 5:24).

He that began a good work in you shall complete it until the day of Christ (Philippians 1:6).

"For the vision *is* yet for an appointed time; But at the end it will speak, and it will not lie. Though it tarries, wait for it; Because it will surely come, It will not tarry" (Habakkuk 2:3).

Faithfulness

Remain Faithful, even when others are not Faithful!

Don't allow offense, hurt, betrayal, disappointment or anything, poison your spirit.

People fail, but God is always faithful! Even when our faith is weak He is always faithful!

2 Timothy 2:13

"If we are faithless, He remains faithful; He cannot deny Himself."

Proverbs 20:6

"Most men will proclaim each his own goodness, But who can find a faithful man?"

Matthew 25:23

"His lord said to him, 'Well done, good and faithful servant; you have been faithful over a few things, I will make you ruler over many things. Enter into the joy of your lord.'"

Be Faithful over the little, so God can make you to rule (as a king) over much.

Faith and patience inherit the promises

Endurance

When we're abiding in Christ through the really difficult things, that's what puts our faith to the test! (Or where the rubber meets the road!) Walking out the word of God, that we're hearing, and being a doer of the Word, (James 1:22).

In our earlier years, as a young family, we had to endure hardship! As many Christian families may not want to admit, there are challenges in the family with finances and raising children throughout all their growing up years and we as parents being in the ministry, there were challenges. We saw our children go through some things even in the church that were sometimes unfair to them and to keep the peace with people, we didn't inquire of "the matters", so they suffered some unfair situations. Looking back, we realized we needed more wisdom in these areas, of how to deal with these types of relationship problems.

Through it all we trusted the Lord to bring us through those "hard places" and learned how to walk in God's unconditional love! We have to admit, it wasn't easy, but through it all, the Lord really taught us wisdom in relationships! He taught us when to say something and when NOT to say something!

James 1:2-4

"My brethren, count it all joy when you fall into various trials, knowing that the testing of your faith produces patience. But let patience have *its* perfect work, that you may be perfect and complete, lacking nothing."

Stick with it attitude!

Have a strong "stick with it attitude." Refuse to bow to the pressure. Refuse to compromise. Refuse to quit. Determine daily, like the Prophet Daniel, who purposed in his heart that he would not defile himself with the king's (devil's) delicacies, that you will not defile yourself with the flesh, the world, the devil. Purpose in your heart to not look back, act back, or compromise the high calling God has on your life! If you focus on Jesus, spend quality time with Jesus daily, He will strengthen you to stay the course and stick with your true God given destiny! Make a decision and determine today that you will not live a mediocre, casual, Christian life. Declare over yourself, "by the Grace of God, I will be obedient to the heavenly vision" (Acts 26:19).

Be a Strong Finisher!

Jesus said to them, "My food is to do the will of Him who sent Me, and to finish His work" (John 4:34).

Hebrews 12:2

God says "looking unto Jesus, the author and finisher of our faith . . ."

Jesus is a finisher! As disciples of Jesus Christ we must determine "that by the grace of God" I will finish God's assignment! I will obey the high calling of God.

In the good times, in the challenging times determine never to quit! Don't quit!

Reflection Scriptures

Joshua 1:9

"Have I not commanded you? Be strong and of good courage; do not be afraid, nor be dismayed, for the LORD your God *is* with you wherever you go."

Isaiah 41:10

"Fear not, for I *am* with you; Be not dismayed, for I am your God. I will strengthen you, Yes, I will help you, I will uphold you with My righteous right hand."

1 Corinthians 9:24

"Do you know that those who run in a race all run, but one receives the prize? Run in such a way that you may obtain *it*."

Ephesians 6:10

"Finally, my brethren, be strong in the Lord and in the power of His might."

2 Timothy 1:7

"For God did not given us a spirit of fear, but of power and of love and of a sound mind."

Psalm 37:24

"Though he fall, he shall not be utterly cast down; For the LORD upholds *him with* his hand."

KEM & DARA GASKIN

Let us pray for you

Father we thank you for the spirit of endurance!!! Grace to endure, grace to overcome, grace to stay the course and possess the promises you have declared over their lives. Father by this are you glorified, that they bear much fruit. We speak life into their spirit, that they shall continue to say yes to you Father, and yes to the "High Call" that you have in their life in Jesus' Name! Let the earth receive the full blessing of the gift that they are to this generation and let millions of souls come to Jesus as a result of their "YES" in Jesus Name! Amen!!!

CONCLUSION

I f we would've quit when it felt like WW3 was happening all around us, then we would not be walking in what God had prophesied many years ago! Our Great God and Faithful Father did it for us and He will do it for you. You're not a quitter, you're a finisher! You're not a spiritual wimp, through Christ you're a mighty warrior! Trust, obey, endure, and finish your Kingdom assignment. Millions of souls are waiting for God's glory to manifest in and through your life! Your destiny has been paid for by the precious Blood of Jesus! Now go lay hold of it, no matter what happens.

#DONTQUIT #SELAH

ACKNOWLEDGMENT

We Thank God for our four beautiful adult children, their spouses and our precious grandchildren. Like many families we have gone through many trials in our family, however God has always been there to keep us! We Love each and every one of them VERY VERY Much! We Thank God that each of our children have faith in Christ and that this legacy of faith and passion for Jesus Christ will continue in our family for many generations to come.

Over the years there have been so many people who have impacted our lives! God gave us some special jewels of Kingdom People at critical times in our lives.

We want to thank Pastors Rich & Sue Ruiz. They were our very first Pastors. surely they were sent by God to help reach us, disciple us, spank us, and love us unconditionally through many situations and trials of life. Through spiritual and financial battles, through the major health crisis with our son, and more Pastors Rich and Sue were there. We thank God for their life and commitment to the Gospel of Jesus Christ.

Also, we thank God for the precious life of Pastor Todd Ruiz who inherited the church from his parents Pastors Rich

& Sue Ruiz. When my wife and I were first saved Pastor Todd was a young and on fire evangelist!!! And OMG, the Lord anointed Pastor Todd to be a mighty voice and a powerful deliverer, to many people young & old. We miss Pastor Todd, as he has already graduated to heaven, but his spirit lives on in many kingdom soldiers doing the work of the ministry today.

Last but definitely not least, we thank God for our Wonderful WHCO Eldership, Leadership and Church Family! In my view these are some of the Most amazing and loyal believers in the Kingdom of God!!! They have prayed with us, stood with us, been in the trenches of spiritual battles with us and by God's Grace this WHCO Family has now become an International Ministry. The vision to preach the Gospel, win millions of souls worldwide, build water wells, build Kingdom Children Orphanages, and shift the future of nations will be fulfilled by the grace of God and the faith of these covenant men and women at WHCO. To God be the Glory Forever for His amazing grace & Glory!

ABOUT THE AUTHOR

Doctors Kem & Dara Gaskin were both saved by the Grace of Jesus Christ in 1988. Then Married in 1989. They have four Children and seven grandchildren! The Lord has blessed Kem & Dara to serve as Senior Leaders and Overseers of 2 active Churches. One in Lancaster, CA and one in Niteroi, Brazil. They have been awarded each with 2 honorary doctorates in Philosophy of Humanities. By God's grace Kem & Dara have preached the Gospel of Jesus Christ in at least 12 different nations believing God for souls saved, revival and reformation. All to the Glory of God Forever!

Here are some pictures from the last 6 years of ministry in our church and several Nations. God is Faithful!

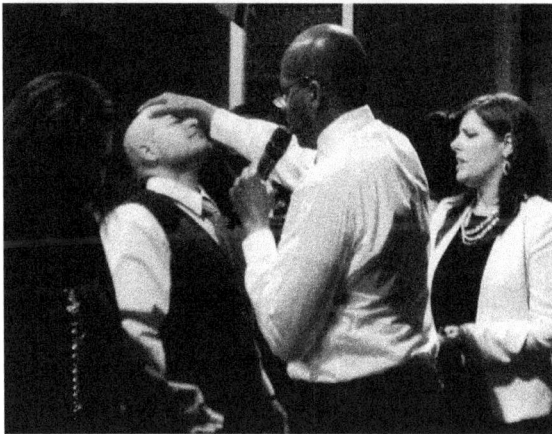

WORLD HARVEST CHRISTIAN OUTREACH

WORLD HARVEST CHRISTIAN OUTREACH

WORLD HARVEST CHRISTIAN OUTREACH

CONTACT INFORMATION

World Harvest Christian Outreach Church

224 West Lancaster Blvd, Lancaster, CA 93534

(661)945-5500

whcoministries.org

facebook@whcoglobal

facebook@whcoministries